1997 Top of the Charts
Arranged by Dan Coates

Project Manager: Carol Cuellar
Book Design: Ken Rehm
©1997 WARNER BROS. PUBLICATIONS
All Rights Reserved

• • • C O N T E N T S • • •

ALL OF MY LIFE

Lyrics by
ALAN and MARILYN BERGMAN

Music by
BARBRA STREISAND and
MARVIN HAMLISCH
Arranged by DAN COATES

BECAUSE YOU LOVED ME
(Theme from "UP CLOSE & PERSONAL")

Words and Music by
DIANE WARREN
Arrnaged by DAN COATES

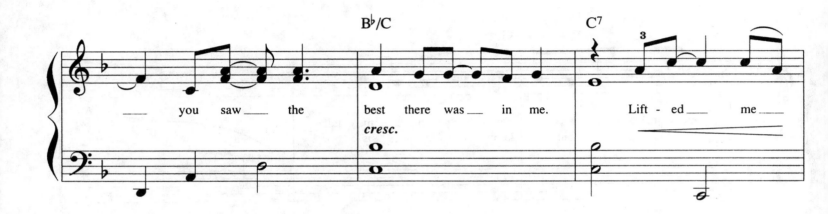

10

BY HEART

Composed by
JIM BRICKMAN and
HOLLYE LEVEN
Arranged by DAN COATES

CHANGE THE WORLD

Words and Music by
TOMMY SIMS, GORDON KENNEDY
and WAYNE KIRKPATRICK
Arranged by DAN COATES

Change the World - 4 - 1

16

Change the World - 4 - 3

HERO'S DREAM

Composed by
JIM BRICKMAN
Arranged by DAN COATES

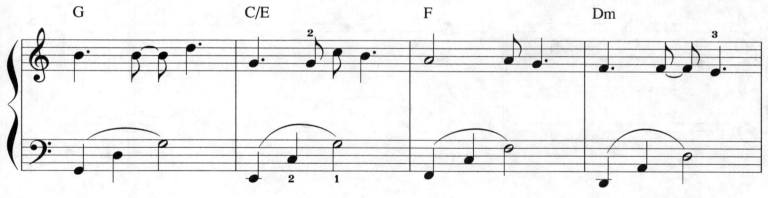

Hero's Dream - 4 - 2

Hero's Dream - 4 - 4

From the Motion Picture "THE PREACHER'S WIFE"

I BELIEVE IN YOU AND ME

Words and Music by
SANDY LINZER and DAVID WOLFERT
Arranged by DAN COATES

24

Verse 2:
I will never leave your side,
I will never hurt your pride.
When all the chips are down,
I will always be around
Just to be right where you are, my love.
Oh, I love you, boy.
I will never leave you out,
I will always let you in
To places no one has ever been.
Deep inside, can't you see?
I believe in you and me.

I BELIEVE I CAN FLY

Words and Music by
R. KELLY
Arranged by DAN COATES

28

From the Motion Picture "THE MIRROR HAS TWO FACES"

I FINALLY FOUND SOMEONE

Written by
BARBRA STREISAND, MARVIN HAMLISCH,
R. J. LANGE and BRYAN ADAMS
Arranged by DAN COATES

I fi - n'lly found some - one that knocks me off of my feet.

I fi - n'lly found the one that makes me feel com - plete.

I Finally Found Someone - 6 - 1

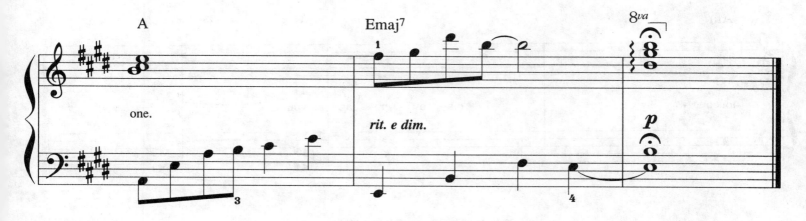

I LOVE YOU ALWAYS FOREVER

Words and Music by
DONNA LEWIS
Arranged by DAN COATES

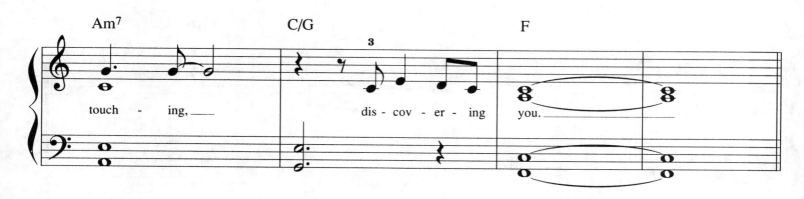

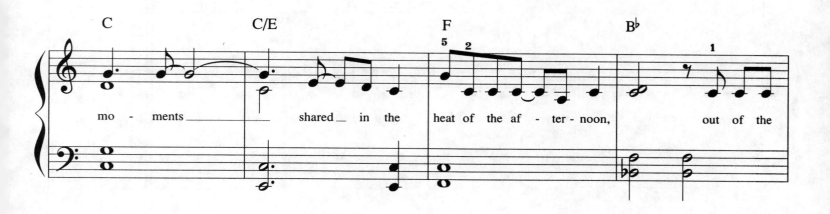

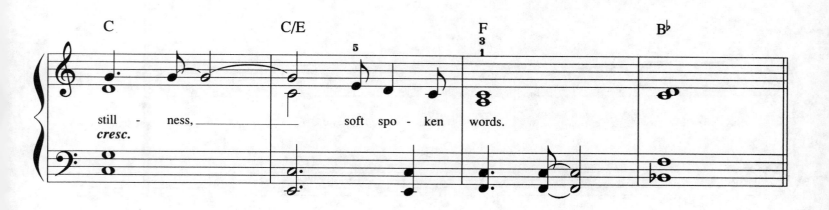

Chorus:

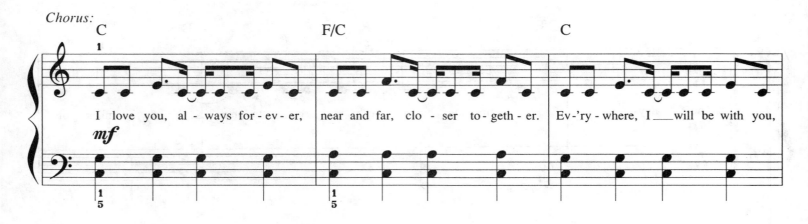

I love you, al - ways for - ev - er, near and far, clo - ser to - geth - er. Ev - 'ry - where, I ___ will be with you,

ev - 'ry - thing, I ___ will do for you. I love you, al - ways for - ev - er, near and far, clo - ser to - geth - er.

Ev - 'ry - where, I ___ will be with you, ev - 'ry - thing, I ___ will do for you. ev - 'ry - thing, I ___ will do for you.

Say you love, love ___ me for - ev - er, nev - er stop, nev - er what - ev - er. Near and far and al - ways and ev - 'ry -

Verse 3:
You've got the most unbelievable blue eyes I've ever seen.
You've got me almost melting away as we lay there
Under blue sky with pure white stars,
Exotic sweetness, a magical time.
(To Chorus:)

COUNT ON ME

Words and Music by
BABYFACE, WHITNEY HOUSTON
and MICHAEL HOUSTON
Arranged by DAN COATES

Count on me ___ through thick and thin, a friend-ship that ___ will nev-er end. When you are weak, ___ I will be strong, help-ing you ___ to car-ry on. ___ Call on me, ___ I will be there. Don't be a-fraid. Please be-lieve ___ me when I say count on. ___

Count on Me - 5 - 1

44

KEY WEST INTERMEZZO
(I SAW YOU FIRST)

Words and Music by
JOHN MELLENCAMP and GEORGE GREEN
Arranged by DAN COATES

Moderate rock ♩ = 116

mf

1. In a hand-painted night, me and Gyp-sy Scot-ty are part-ners

at the Ho-tel Fla-min-go, wear-ing black-mar-ket

shoes. This loud Cu-ban band

46

48

Verse 3:
On a moon spattered road in her parrot rebozo,
Gypsy Scotty is driving his big, long, yellow car.
She flies like a bird over his shoulder.
She whispers in his ear, "Boy, you are my star."
(To Chorus:)

Verse 4:
In the bone colored dawn, me and Gypsy Scotty are singin',
The radio is playing, she left her shoes out in the back.
He tells me a story about some girl he knows in Kentucky.
He just made that story up, there ain't no girl like that.
(To Chorus:)

MACARENA

Words and Music by
ANTONIO ROMERO
and RAFAEL RUIZ
Arranged by DAN COATES

grí - a Ma - ca - re - na que tu cuer - po_es pa' dar - le_a - le - grí - a_y co - sa - bue - na.

Da - le_a tu cuer - po_a - le - grí - a Ma - ca - re - na, eh, Ma - ca - re - na. Ma - ca-

G

re - na tie - ne_un no - vio que se lla - ma, que se lla - ma de_a - pe - lli - do Vi - to-

ri - no. Y_en la ju - ra de ban - de - ra del mu - cha - cho

53

Macarena - 4 - 4

ONE OF US

Words and Music by
ERIC BAZILIAN
Arranged by DAN COATES

God had a name,___ what would it be and would you call it to his face,
God had a face,___ what would it look like and would you want to see,

One of Us - 4 - 1

One of Us - 4 - 2

56

One of Us - 4 - 3

KILLING ME SOFTLY
(WITH HIS SONG)

Words by
NORMAN GIMBLE

Music by
CHARLES FOX
Arranged by DAN COATES

Verse:

1. I heard he sang a good song, I heard he had a style.
2. I felt all flushed with fe-ver, em-bar-rassed by the crowd.

And so I came to see him to lis-ten for a while.
I felt he found my let-ters and read each one out loud.

And there he was this young boy, a stran-ger to my eyes.
I prayed that he would fin-ish, but he just kept right on.

Chorus:

Strum-ming my pain with his fin-gers, sing-ing my life with his words.

Killing Me Softly - 3 - 2

Verse 3:
He sang as if he knew me,
In all my dark despair.
And then he looked right through me
As if I wasn't there.
But he was there, this stranger
Singing clear and strong. (To Chorus:)

REACH

Words and Music by
GLORIA ESTEFAN and
DIANE WARREN
Arranged by DAN COATES

62

64

SEND ME A LOVER

Words and Music by
RICHARD HAHN and
GEORGE THATCHER
Arranged by DAN COATES

I was - n't search - ing
It still as - tounds me,

to end this hurt - ing,
the way you found me,

but out of no - where you made me
it's al - most too good   to be

feel.
true.

I cried a - bout it,
From our first meet - ing,

I lied a - bout it,
I had the feel - ing

and tried to doubt this could be
the rest of my life I'd spend with

real.
you.

You've touched me far too deep for
I   just can't turn my back on

68

From the Twentieth Century Fox Motion Picture
THAT THING YOU DO!

Words and Music by
ADAM SCHLESINGER
Arranged by DAN COATES

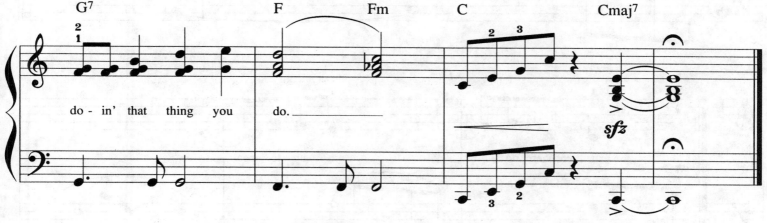

Verse 2:
I know all the games you play.
And I'm gonna find a way to let you know
That you'll be mine someday.
'Cause we could be happy, can't you see?
If you'd only let me be the one to hold you
And keep you here with me.
'Cause I try and try to forget you, girl,
But it's just too hard to do.
Every time you do that thing you do.

Verse 3:
(8 Bar Instrumental Solo...)
'Cause we could be happy, can't you see?
If you'd only let me be the one to hold you
And keep you here with me.
'Cause it hurts me so just to see you go
Around with someone new.
(To Coda:)

VALENTINE

Composed by
JIM BRICKMAN and JACK KUGELL
Arranged by DAN COATES

Moderately slow (♩ = 92)

75

Valentine - 4 - 2

D.S. 𝄋 al Coda

And

Verse 2:
All of my life,
I have been waiting for all you give to me.
You've opened my eyes
And shown me how to love unselfishly.
I've dreamed of this a thousand times before,
But in my dreams I couldn't love you more.
I will give you my heart until the end of time.
You're all I need, my love,
My Valentine.

YOU'LL SEE

Words and Music by
MADONNA CICCONE and
DAVID FOSTER
Arranged by DAN COATES

80

You'll See - 4 - 3

Verse 2:
You think that I can never laugh again,
You'll see.
You think that you've destroyed my faith in love.
You think after all you've done,
I'll never find my way back home.
You'll see, somehow, some day.   (To Chorus:)

Verse 3:
You think that you are strong, but you are weak,
You'll see.
It takes more strength to cry, admit defeat.
I have truth on my side,
You only have deceit.
You'll see, somehow, some day.   (To Chorus:)

UN-BREAK MY HEART

Words and Music by
DIANE WARREN
Arranged by DAN COATES

One of today's foremost personalities in the field of printed music, Dan Coates has been providing teachers and professional musicians with quality piano material since 1975. Equally adept in arranging for beginners or accomplished musicians, his Big Note, Easy Piano and Professional Touch arrangements have made a significant contribution to the industry.

Born in Syracuse, New York, Dan began to play piano at age four. By the time he was 15, he'd won a New York State competition for music composers. After high school graduation, he toured the United States, Canada and Europe as an arranger and pianist with the world-famous group "Up With People".

Dan settled in Miami, Florida, where he studied piano with Ivan Davis at the University of Miami while playing professionally throughout southern Florida. To date, his performance credits include appearances on "Murphy Brown," "My Sister Sam" and at the Opening Ceremonies of the 1984 Summer Olympics in Los Angeles. Dan has also accompanied such artists as Dusty Springfield and Charlotte Rae.

In 1982, Dan began his association with Warner Bros. Publications - an association which has produced more than 400 Dan Coates books and sheets. Throughout the year he conducts piano workshops nation-wide, during which he demonstrates his popular arrangements.

ENJOY THESE PIANO ARRANGEMENT BOOKS
FROM DAN COATES

FOR BIG NOTE PIANO

I Swear and 10 Top
Country Hits (PF0888)

FOR EASY PIANO

Biggest Hits of the '80's & '90's
(Revised & Updated) (PF0850)

Biggest Hits of 1993-1994
(PF0893)

Dan Coates' Golden Collection
of 50 Broadway Blockbusters
(PF0917)

Dan Coates' Golden Collection
of 50 Movie Themes (PF0915)

Dreamlover & 15 Contemporary
Love Songs (PF0884)

Hero & 12 Great Ballads
(PF0899)

How Do You Keep the Music
Playing? & 15 Great Movie
Songs (PF0926)

I Cross My Heart + 12 Top Hits
(PF0902)

I Swear and 8 Top Country Hits
(PF0911)

Superheroes and Cartoon
Superstars (PF0880)

Top of the Charts, 1994
Edition, Volume 1 (PF0919)

Top of the Charts, 1993
Edition, Volume 2 (PF0883)

LISTEN & PLAY SERIES
FOR EASY PIANO

Broadway Today
Book and Cassette (PF0885)

Great Songs from the Movies
Book and Cassette (PF0886)

FOR INTERMEDIATE/
ADVANCED PIANO DUET

7 Golden Hits (PF0918)
(1 Piano - 4 Hands)

MY FAVORITE CLASSICS
SERIES

My Favorite Classics
52 Piano Solos
(Revised Edition)
compiled and edited by
Dan Coates (PF0909)